THE FITZWILLIAM VIRGINAL BOOK

EDITED FROM THE ORIGINAL MANUSCRIPT
WITH AN INTRODUCTION AND NOTES
BY
J. A. FULLER MAITLAND
AND
W. BARCLAY SQUIRE

Revised Dover Edition
Corrected, Edited and with a Preface by
BLANCHE WINOGRON

In Two Volumes
VOLUME II

DOVER PUBLICATIONS, INC.
NEW YORK

Published in Canada by General Publishing Company, Ltd.,
30 Lesmill Road, Don Mills, Toronto, Ontario.
Published in the United Kingdom by Constable and Company, Ltd.

The Revised Dover Edition, first published in 1979–80, is an
unabridged republication of the work originally published in
1899 by Breitkopf and Härtel that incorporates numerous corrections by Blanche Winogron.
Miss Winogron has written a Preface especially for the Dover
Edition in which she comments on the corrections. In order to
make room for this new material it was necessary to delete the
German translation of the Notes to Volume II from the original
text.

International Standard Book Number: 0-486-21069-3
Library of Congress Catalog Card Number: 63-19495

Manufactured in the United States of America
Dover Publications, Inc.
180 Varick Street
New York, N.Y. 10014

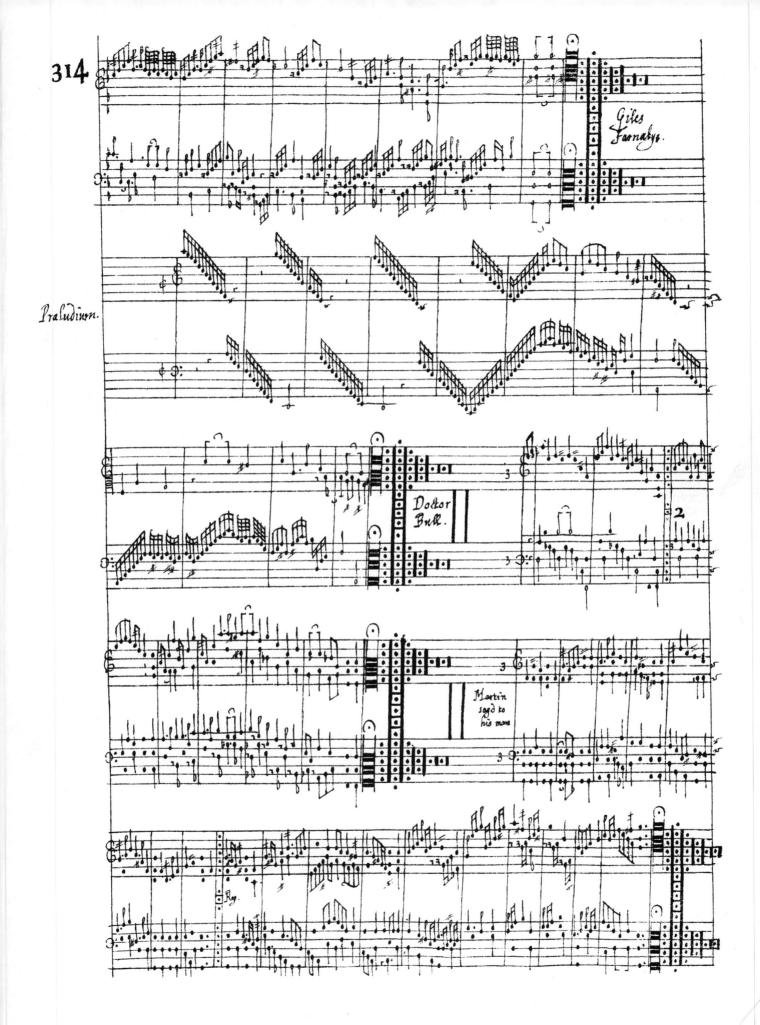

CONTENTS OF VOL. II.

NOTE. The Roman numbers in square brackets, refer to the modes. See Introduction, vol. i, p. XII.

PREFACE TO THE REVISED DOVER EDITION

It is almost eighty years since the distinguished music critic of the London Times, John Alexander Fuller Maitland, and his brother-in-law William Barclay Squire, critic, editor and music librarian of the British Museum, published their impressive transcription of *The Fitzwilliam Virginal Book*. They carried off their difficult task with an astonishing degree of skill and accuracy—a truly monumental accomplishment for the time. Interest in the great *corpus* of English Renaissance music was just beginning; the science of musicology was in its infancy. Impetus for the project may have come from the pioneering activities of Arnold Dolmetsch, a gifted and dynamic Swiss musician, craftsman and indefatigable researcher in early music, newly established in England, whose followers among distinguished musicians, writers and artists included Fuller Maitland. The latter had evidently become an enthusiastic supporter, and a convert to the harpsichord (even to performing in occasional concerts), perhaps inspired by his first acquaintance with the great body of virginal music in the Fitzwilliam Museum uncovered in the process of preparing that institution's music catalog, completed in 1887.

With the tremendous upsurge in the performance of Renaissance and Baroque music in the past forty years, and the serious study of early instruments and their literatures, *The Fitzwilliam Virginal Book* has become recognized as the treasure house of a most sophisticated keyboard music. Highly developed and idiomatic in style, the book is now generally acknowledged to be the foundation for all keyboard music which followed it in the next two centuries. This remarkable collection also serves as an important historical document reflecting the musical life of the time; from this source a large part of English music in many of its facets and forms (including that of the theater) from the 1560s to 1620 could be reconstructed.

Although the Maitland–Squire text has long been accepted as a faithful translation into modern notation (two reprints of the original edition have appeared in the last twenty or more years), a growing number of active performers and scholars have felt that the correction of obvious errors, oversights and misprints (perhaps due to insufficient proofreading) would make it ever more useful. Such lapses were, of course, inevitable considering the enormity and complexity of the publication. However, it was only after a thoroughgoing critical reexamination of the entire collection was undertaken by the present Editor,

with a copy of the original manuscript and a pair of virginals at hand, that the full extent and nature of these corrections was realized. There were not only innumerable "lapses," but a considerable number of misreadings and misinterpretations of the manuscript previously unsuspected. Nevertheless a completely new publication was not warranted; needed revision could be successfully accomplished by incorporating the corrections into the existing volumes without altering the basic text, editorial policy or printing style, an operation fortunately made possible by the economical procedures of modern photolithography.

Corrections and changes in this revised edition stem from errors which fall into three categories: those originating with the scribe, those of the printer, and editorial errors in transcription. In the first category we find (a) placement of notes on wrong lines or spaces (a mistake easily made on a six-line staff); wrong placement or omission of clefs and clef changes, or places where these were written so small as to be missed even by the magnifying glass, causing several passages to be transcribed a third too high, too low or in the wrong range (see for example, Volume I, page 66, line 5, measure 2; page 190, line 4, measure 3; Volume II, page 244, line 3, measure 2); (b) many rhythmic and chromatic ambiguities caused by crowding within the measure; omission of dots, stems, tails; uncompleted melodic lines (Volume II, page 39, line 3, measure 1); some illegibility due to age or smudging; and the very nature of the notation itself (see the Introduction, Volume I, pages XI and XII). Printer's errors include occasional omission of, or wrongly placed, modern clefs, fingering, accidentals, stemming, beaming, dots, rests, a few ornaments, some poor alignments, uncompleted melodic lines (sometimes even within a *cantus*—Volume I, page 181, line 3, measure 1).

In a number of cases of editorial misreadings or misinterpretations of notes, rhythms in the manuscript demanded major reconstruction (one or two measures in each instance). The more important of these are: Volume I—page 4, line 5, measure 2; page 20, line 2, measure 4; page 130, line 5, measure 3; page 142, line 2, measure 3; page 171, line 5, measures 2, 3; Volume II—page 23, line 5, measure 1; page 93, line 5, measure 2, line 6, measure 1; page 99, line 3, measure 3; page 265, line 2, measure 1; page 340, line 5, measure 4, line 6, measure 1.

In addition to restoring the many omitted notes (chord

tones, melodic lines), chords, accidentals, rests, and the supplying of editorial brackets and correcting of a few misplaced fingerings, the present Editor has also righted a number of musical decisions (some of them untenable in the light of present-day knowledge) and has clarified occasional confusion among rests, inkblots and *directs*. Indications for triplets and sextolets have been reduced to a minimum for ease of reading, their slurs removed, except when necessary for clarity. Numerals indicating voice entrances in several of the five *Ut, re, mi* pieces have been reduced in size for the sake of consistency and to avoid mistaking them for fingering or numbering of strains. All editorial additions and corrections, except for restoration of what was originally in the manuscript, are bracketed or have footnotes. To preserve the modality of the time, some editorial accidentals have been eliminated and others suggested in parentheses.

Unnecessary footnotes have been emended. In a few places, due to *lacunae* or illegibility of the manuscript, the missing material has been supplied by collation with other manuscripts and is so indicated in footnotes. All fingering is original, a fact only hinted at in the Introduction.

As for the manuscript's elaborate double bars, the original editors recognized their probable decorative function (see the Introduction, Volume I, pages XVI and XVII), but unfortunately decided to include them as repeat signs. They are obviously redundant in the strain and variation form (also traditional in the solo lute and consort music of the time), and have been eliminated throughout except in the short bipartite dances and character pieces without variation, where repeats seem to be called for. In the latter cases, the player may improvise his own simple embellishments. Due to the problem of limited space, first and second endings may not always make mathematical sense when an upbeat is involved; but the player can easily make the necessary adjustment. Final *breve* chords have been retained, since they are more often than not a part of the structural rhythmic pulse.

With reference to the Tregian family connection elaborated on in the Introduction (see pp. VI–IX), the Editor would like to call attention to the most recent findings as published in *Music and Letters:* Cole, Elizabeth, "In Search of Francis Tregian" *(Music and Letters,* XXXIII, 1952, p. 28); Schofield, B. and Dart, T., "Tregian's Anthology" *(Music and Letters,* XXXII, 1951, pp. 205–16).

The critical note to page 373 in Volume I, page XXVI, referring to the *Toccata* of Giovanni Picchi, "This absurd piece of music, by an Italian composer otherwise unknown . . ." should be amended. Picchi (fl. early 17th century) is known to have been organist at the Chiesa Della Casa Grande in Venice. The *Toccata* which represents him in this collection, although not one of his great pieces, is obviously modeled after those of Girolamo Frescobaldi (1583–1643) with whom he probably studied. Picchi's very fine set of twelve dances for keyboard, the *Intavolatura d'Arpicordo* (Venice, 1620), includes a *Pass'e mezzo Antico* and its *Saltarello,* a *Polachca,* two Hungarian dances and a German *Todesca.* He also wrote vocal music, both sacred and secular, and three *Sonatas* for violins and wind instruments.

BLANCHE WINOGRON

January, 1979

NOTES*) TO VOLUME II.

P. 1. See note to vol. i. p. 427. A copy of this setting, entitled "Felix nunquam", is in Forster, p. 24, with no composer's name to it; and another is in Cosyns, p. 150.

P. 12. The exercise marked CXI, has neither clefs, time-signature, nor indications as to key. The notes have no tails. No. CXII has nothing in common with "Tell mee, Daphne", on p. 446 of this volume.

P. 19. See Chappell, pp. 456, 782, 794.

P. 22. In Ward's List.

P. 23. The abbreviation "Dor.", cannot refer to the Dorian mode, as this prelude is in the transposed Ionian mode (XIII*). See note on vol. i, pp. 129 and 177. This prelude can hardly be connected with the pavan and galliard, nos. XXXIV and XLVIII, as the mode is altogether different.

P. 34. This extraordinary experiment in rhythm is marked only with the barred semicircle, and the arrangement of bars is as indicated by the continuous lines: the dotted lines are supplied until the bottom line of p. 35, when the arrangement of the MS. is followed, marking off, as it were, a little bar of 3—4 time from the larger bar of 8—4 time. Later on, from p. 37, line 3 onwards, the larger bar is divided into two halves of common time, an arrangement which holds good until p. 39, when each of the crotchets is

*) LIST OF BOOKS REFERRED TO IN THE NOTES.

Add. MSS. Additional Manuscripts in the British Museum, London.

CHAPPELL. "The Ballad Literature and Popular Music of the Olden Time; a History of the Ancient Songs, Ballads, and the Dance Times of England, with numerous Anectodes and entire Ballads. Also a Short Account of the Minstrels. By W. Chappell, F. S. A. The whole of the Airs harmonized by G. A. Macfarren." (No date.)

COSYNS. Benjamin Cosyns' Virginal Book, a MS. volume in Her Majesty's Library at Buckingham Palace.

FORSTER. Will. Forster's Virginal Book, another MS. volume in the Buckingham Palace Library, dated 1624.

NEVELL. My Lady Nevell's Booke, a MS. collection of Virginal music in the possession of the Marquess of Abergavenny, copied by J. Baldwine of Windsor in 1591.

WARD. Lives of the Gresham Professors, by John Ward (1740), containing a list of Virginal Compositions by Dr. John Bull, who was the first Gresham Professor of Music, from 1596 to 1607.

divided into three quavers. It is worth noticing how truly the rhythm is kept throughout the piece.

P. 42. The theme of this piece is the famous "Lachrymae" of John Dowland, (Second Booke of Songs or Ayres, 1600); it next appears in "Lachrymae, or Seven Teares, figured in seven passionate Pavans, set forth for the lute, viols, or violins, in five parts", in 1605. The first of the seven is the work which is constantly alluded to as "Lachrymae". Add. MS. 31,392 fol. 35 b has Dowland's "Lachrymae" in lute tablature. The tune is to be found in nearly every Elizabethan collection. It occurs at fol. 71a of Add. MS. 30,485, and a setting by Cosyns is in his book, p. 8. See Chappell, p. 92. A setting by Morley is in this volume, p. 173, and one by Giles Farnaby at p. 472.

P. 47. The piece occurs as "Hardings Galliard", without Byrd's name, in Forster, p. 380. Two "fancies" by James Harding are in Add. MS. 30,485, f. 47 and 50.

P. 54. Some marginal notes on p. 226 of the MS. possibly referring to section 3 of this piece, have been rendered illegible by the binder.

P. 64. In Ward's list.

P. 67. A copy is in Nevell, fol. 113 a.

P. 77. The same tune set by Munday, occurs in vol. i. p. 66. See Chappell, p. 233. In Add. MS. 23,623 fol. 13b, it is given as "Bonni well Robin van Doct. Jan Bull".

P. 87. See foot-notes at the end of the piece; the last ten bars are evidently meant to be played *at libitum*, as some of them contain five crotchets, others six, and the majority four. The work is an interesting example of a ground kept nearly always in the highest part, and beginning with a simple statement of the theme with a pause marked after it.

P. 94. A different setting from the anonymous treatment of the same tune, vol. i. p. 72.

P. 103. A copy of this setting is in Forster, p. 288. See vol. i. p. 99 ff., which has been used in correcting the corrupt bars noted on pp. 104 and 106. These stand in the MS. thus:

P. 104. sect. 2. bars 6,7:

Pag. 106. Sect. 4 bars 7 and 8 right hand:

See vol. i. p. 99 ff.

P. 110. The foot-note [**] refers only to the left-hand part of the penultimate bar.

P. 111. A copy is in Forster, p. 302.

P. 116. In Ward's list. A composition on the same theme, by Cosyns, is in his book p. 75.

P. 119. Line three in the last group of semiquavers in the left hand, the C should be marked natural.

P. 121. In Ward's list.

P. 125. In Ward's list.

P. 128. In Ward's list. The piece occurs also as "Courante Juweel", with slight differences in Add. MS. 23,623, fol. 70b, where there is besides another setting, (at fol. 49b) entitled "Het Juweel van Doctor Jan Bull quod fecit anno 1621, 12. December." A slightly different version occurs in Cosyns, p. 124.

P. 131. In Ward's list. See Chappell, pp. 240, 776.

P. 135. The composer was probably either Robert Parsons (d. 1570) or his son John (d. 1623). The only entry is the name "Persons" at the end of the piece.

P. 138. The figure after the title, here given as "2", should be "11" as marking the eleventh of Farnaby's pieces in the collection. See Chappell, p. 793.

P. 146. In Ward's list.

P. 148. Bull's setting of this beautiful tune is in Add. MS. 23,623 fol. 17b, where it is called "Rose a solis van Joan Bull Doct.".

P. 161. The theme of this piece became popular later as a catch, "Slaves to the world", which is ascribed to Edmund Nelham in the second edition of Hilton's 'Catch that Catch can' (1658.)

P. 166. See Chappell, p. 74.

P. 173. This is another setting of Dowland's "Lachrymae", though there is no acknowledgment of the fact in the MS. See note to p. 42.

P. 180. This piece occurs under the name "Levalto" in Forster, p. 20.

P. 184. See Chappell, p. 86.

P. 186. See Chappell, p. 793. The tune, the Irish origin of which is denoted by its name ("Colleen oge asthore") is referred to by Shakespeare, Henry V., IV. iv. 4. See also the New English Dictionary, s. v. CALINO. Another copy is in Add. MS. 30,485, fol. 96b.

P. 190. See Chappell, pp. 114 and 770. The piece occurs under the name "Lord Willobies welcome home", in Nevell, fol. 146b, and Forster, p. 22. Against the bass line

at the beginning is written in the margin "300* to S. T. by Tom".

P. 192. Another setting of this tune is at p. 462 of this volume.

P. 234. See Chappell, pp. 123, and 771. Another copy is in Cosyns. p. 46, where it is signed with his initials.

P. 236. "The Irishe Dumpe" is referred to in Chappell, p. 793. "Watkins Ale" occurs also in Forster, p. 460. See Chappell, p. 136.

P. 242. In Ward's list.

P. 244. In Ward's list.

P. 248. The significance of the initial D cannot be shown; it can have nothing to do with the mode or key of the piece. In Ward's list.

P. 249. In Ward's list.

P. 251. In Ward's list.

P. 258. It is practically certain that the "W. B." of "Sr. John Grayes Galiard" is William Byrd. The initials are placed at a sufficient distance apart in the MS. for the name to be added in full, and a similar contraction occurs in other MSS.

P. 259. In Ward's list.

P. 260. No. CXCIII, occurs again, as a "Corranto" at p. 267, No. CCIV. The harmonies are a little less meagre in this version; the only important difference is in line 2, bar 2, left hand, which stands a fifth higher in the other version.

P. 267. See previous note.

P. 268. The melody of the "Daunce" is that given as "Dulcina" in Giles Earle s Song Book, 1626; see Wooldridge's edition of Chappell's "Old English Popular Music" vol. i. p. 160.

P. 270. In the margin are some words which Chappell reads as "R. Rysd. silas."

P. 273. The facsimile frontispiece to this volume contains the passage from line 3, bar 3 of this page, to the end of no. CCXII, on p. 276.

P. 274. In Ward's list.

P. 275 See Chappell, p. 76.

P. 281. In Ward's list, where it is called "Fantasia with 23 Variations upon *Ut, re, mi, fa, sol, fa*".

P. 298. See Chappell, pp. 171, 772.

P. 305. The name at the end of this corranto appears as "William Byrd, sett." but no other composer's name appears to indicate whether the transcription or the theme is assigned to Byrd. The theme is clearly an adaptation of the pavan "Belle qui tiens ma vie", which appears in Thoinot Arbeau's "Orchésographie" (1588) and in many modern collections.

P. 317. See Chappell, pp. 173, 708, 772.

P. 360. See Chappell, pp. 196, 773.

P. 402. This composition occurs, as "The Marche before the Batell" in Nevell, fol. 13b.

P. 406. In the margin is written "Vide P. Philippi sopr. la medesima fuga, p. 158". This refers to the fact that Peter Philips's Fantasia, no. LXXXIV (vol. i, p. 335) is built upon the same subject. Against the third line is written a sentence of which only these words can be read: "la fuga . . . fuggira". This corresponds to the bottom of p. 406 of this volume, and, taken in connection with the fact that the numbers relating to the fugal entries stop at this point, it may be assumed that the sentence drew attention to the free construction of the fantasia from this point onwards, when new "points" or "fugues" are introduced.

P. 412. In Ward's list. "Brunswick's Toy", in Cosyns, p. 114 b, has nothing in common with them.

P. 427. The ornaments of this piece, and the slight alterations of the notes, make the canon not quite clear. It is between the two highest parts, and is at the interval of a fifth below, at the distance of two semibreves. This arrangement of the parts continues strictly to within nine bars of the end, and beside the parts in canon, there are many points of imitation.

P. 430. Another setting by Byrd, of the tune known also as "The Hunt's Up". See vol. i, p. 218. See Chappell, p. 196, and for another copy, Nevell. fol. 46.

P. 442. In Ward's list.
P. 446. See Chappell, p. 158.
P. 447. See Chappell, pp. 177, 789.
P. 445. Line 2, bar 1, left hand, the last note has in the MS. been corrected from *A*, in order to avoid making octaves with the plain-song.

P. 450. Philip Rosseter published a volume of "Ayres" in 1601 and another of "Consort Lessons" in 1609.

P. 459 bottom line. In the MS. opposite this passage is written, "Vedi Mor. 287". This refers to a curious piece of plagiarism, section 3 of Morley's pavan (vol. i, p. 212), being nearly identical with Farnaby's third section.

P. 462. See note on p. 192. A setting of this tune, signed "B. C." is in Cosyns, p. 59, and another, by John Bull, is in Add. MS 30,485, fol. 95 b.

P. 472. See note on p. 42, ante.

P. 481. An anonymous setting of this tune is in vol. i. p. 74.

P. 485. Line 2. At the double bar, which comes at the bottom of p. 411 of the MS., appears the direction "Verte".

P. 489. The curious combination of two rhythms is carried on until line 5 of p. 491. It is evident that the notes of the canto fermo are of equal value, in other words that each bar is of the same duration. In playing the piece it would be incorrect to give the crotchets the same value throughout, and in the MS. the semibreves are never dotted, being divided into six or four crotchets indifferently.

P. 492, bottom line. The five bars comprising this line are misplaced in the MS., and their order is corrected by means of the figures "1, 3, 4. 2, 5", under the bars as they stand written, indicating the order as given here.

P. 494. See Chappell, p. 23.

[CX.]
Felix Namque.
2.

THOMAS TALLIS.

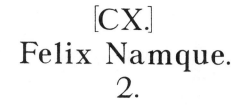

* Minim in the M.S.
Halbe Note in der Handschrift.

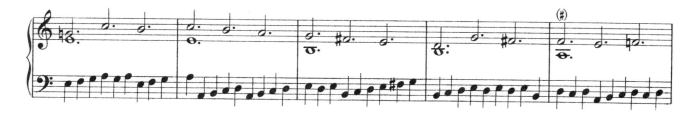

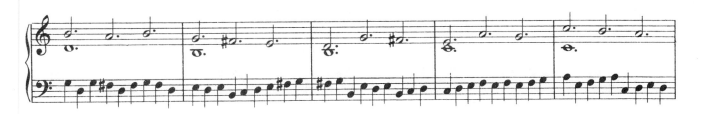

THOMAS TALLIS. 1564.

[CXI.]

ANON. *

[CXII.]
Daphne.
5.

GILES FARNABY.

* This little exercise in three-part counterpoint has no clef or time signature, nor have the notes any tails.
  Dieses kleine, im 3fachen Contrapunkt gesetzte Übungsstück ist ohne Schlüssel und Taktangabe, die Noten sind durchweg ungestielt.

-- Crotchets and Quavers in M. S.
Viertel und Achtel in der Handschrift.

16

GILES FARNABIE.

[CXIII.]
Pawles Wharfe.
6.

GILES FARNABY.

GILES FARNABY.

[CXIV.]
Quodlings Delight.
7.

GILES FARNABY.

*C♯ in the M S.
Cis in der Handschrift.

*F in the M S.
F in der Handschrift.

GILES FARNABY.

[CXV.]
Præludium.

JOHN BULL.

DOCTOR BULL.

[CXVI.]

Præludium. Dor.

John Bull.

* G in the MS.
  G in der Handschrift.

DOCTOR BULL.

[CXVII.]

Præludium.

ANON.

[CXVIII.]

Ut, re, mi, fa, sol, la. a 4 voci.
2.

J. P. SWEELINCK.

* Crotchets in M.S.
  Viertel in der Handschrift.

*Semiquavers in M S.

Sechzehntel in der Handschrift.

*E in the M S.
 E in der Handschrift.

30

*Quaver in M S.
 Achtel in der Handschrift.

*Semiquavers in M S.
Sechzehntel in der Handschrift.

JEHAN PETERSON SWELLING. 1612.

[CXIX.]
In Nomine.

JOHN BULL.

* G sharp in the MS. ** Crotchet in MS. *** Crotchet and 2 quavers in MS.
Gis in der Handschrift. Viertel in der Handschrift. Viertel und 2 Achtel in der Handschrift.

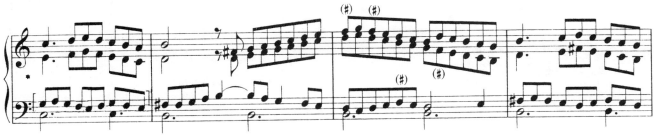

DOCTOR BULL.

* Evidently omitted by clerical error and is here supplied from a copy in Oxford, Christ Church.
Augenscheinlich ist durch ein Schreibfehler, etwas ausgelassen, und ist hier nach einer Handschrift zu
Oxford, Christ Church ergänzt.

[CXX.]
Præludium.

ANON.

[CXXI.]
Pavana Lachrymæ.

JOHN DOWLAND, set by BYRD.

44

* The middle note of this chord is F in the M S.
Die Handschrift hat im Alt F statt E.

Rep.

JHON DOWLAND, sett
foorth by WILLIAM BYRD.

[CXXII.]
Galiarda.

JAMES HARDING, set by BYRD.

Rep.

Rep.

JAMES HARDING, sett
foorth by WILLIAM BYRD.

[CXXIII.]
Pavana.
I.

Thomas Tomkins.

˙) Demisemiquavers in the M.S.
Zweiunddreissigstel in der Handschrift.

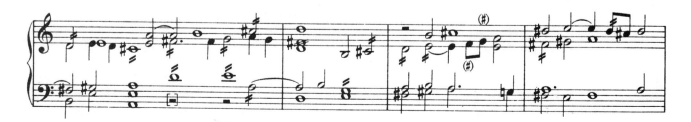

Rep.

* B in M. S.
  H in der Handschrift.

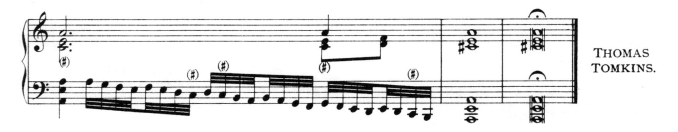

THOMAS
TOMKINS.

[CXXIV.]
Fantasia.

T. MORLEY.

58

* A change of clef is omitted here.
Hier fehlt ein Wechsel des Schlüssels.

THOMAS MORLEY.

* The middle note of this chord is G in the M.S.
In der Handschrift heisst die mittlere Note dieses Accords G.

[CXXV.]
Christe Redemptor.

JOHN BULL.

* An F appears above this D in the M.S.
  In der Handschrift steht über diesem D ein F.

DOCTOR BULL.

* B in the M. S.
H in der Handschrift.

[CXXVI.]
The Maydens Song.

WILLIAM BYRD.

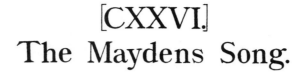

(b)

* Only the last two entries of the subject are numbered in the M. S.
   Nur die beiden letzten Eintritte des Themas sind in der Handschrift nummerirt.

WILLIAM BYRD.

[CXXVII.]
Put up thy Dagger, Jemy.

8

GILES FARNABY.

* F sharp in the M. S.
  Fis in der Handschrift.
** This group consists of 4 quavers and a crotchet in the M. S., evidently by mistake.
  Diese Gruppe besteht in der Handschrift aus 4 Achteln und einem Viertel; offenbar ein Irrthum.

GILES
FARNABY.

* Demisemiquavers in the M. S.
 Zweiunddreissigstel in der Handschrift.

[CXXVIII.]
Bony sweet Robin.
9.

GILES FARNABY.

* Quaver in the M.S.
  Achtel in der Handschrift.

** Quavers in the M.S.
   Achtel in der Handschrift.

* Quavers in the M.S.
  Achtel in der Handschrift.

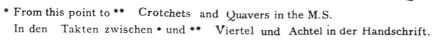

* From this point to ** Crotchets and Quavers in the M.S.
  In den Takten zwischen * und ** Viertel und Achtel in der Handschrift.

GILES
FARNABY.

[CXXIX.]
Fantasia.
10.

GILES FARNABY.

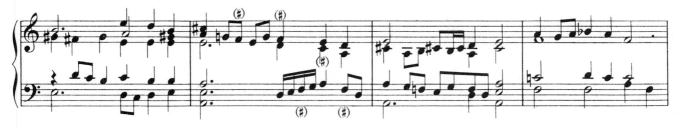

* A in the M. S.
A in der Handschrift.

86

GILES
FARNABY.

* B in the M. S.
  H in der Handschrift.

- - These two bars are omitted from their proper place in the M. S., and added at the foot of the page, with a sign to indi_
cate the place to which they belong.
  Diese beiden Takte sind in der Handschrift an der richtigen Stelle weggelassen und am Fusse der Seite, mit einem hin_
weisenden Zeichen versehen, angefügt.

[CXXX.]
A Grounde.
2.

THOMAS TOMKINS.

- - Semiquavers in the M. S.
    Sechzehntel in der Handschrift.

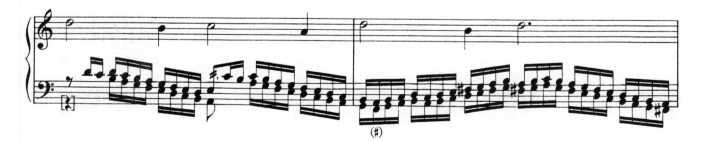

(♯)

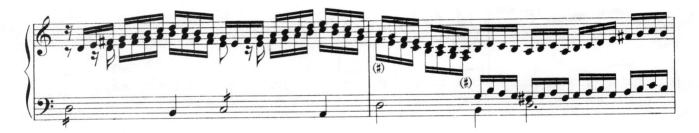

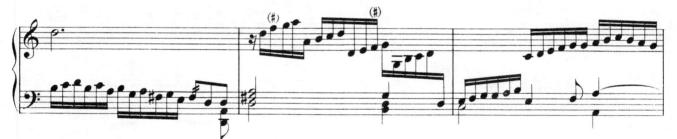

* Crotchet in the M. S.
Viertel in der Handschrift.

* From this point to ** the right hand part in the M.S. is arranged in four groups of triplets, and the bass part of the succeding bar is similarly written.

In den 3 Takten zwischen * und ** ist die Partie der rechten Hand in der Handschrift in 4 Gruppen von Triolen angeordnet; die linke Hand im nächstfolgenden Takte ist in ähnlicher Weise geschrieben.

** Crotchet in the M.S.
   Viertel in der Handschrift.

THOMAS
TOMKINS.

* Semiquavers in the M. S.   ** E in the M. S.   *** Dotted crotchet and Semiquavers in the M.S.
   Sechzehntel in der Handschrift.   E in der Handschrift.   Viertel mit Punkt und Sechzehntel in der Handschrift.

- - Semiquavers in the M. S.
      Sechzehntel in der Handschrift.

[CXXXI.]
Barafostus Dreame.
3.

THOMAS TOMKINS.

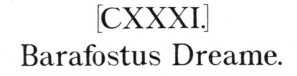

* A, quaver B, in the M. S.
Achtel (H) in der Handschrift.

*- -*Quavers in the M. S.
    Achtel in der Handschrift.
     ** Demisemiquavers in the M.S.
     Zweiunddreissigstel in der Handschrift.

THOMAS
TOMKINS.

∗---∗ Dotted crotchets in the M. S.
Viertel mit Punkt in der Handschrift.

‡ Minims in the M. S.
Halbe Noten in der Handschrift.

[CXXXII.]
The Hunting Galliard.
4.

THOMAS TOMKINS.

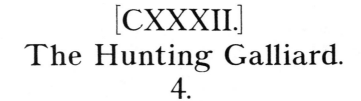

Rep.

* C sharp in the M.S.
  Cis in der Handschrift.

Rep.

THOMAS
TOMKINS.

[CXXXIII.]
The Quadran Paven.

WILLIAM BYRD.

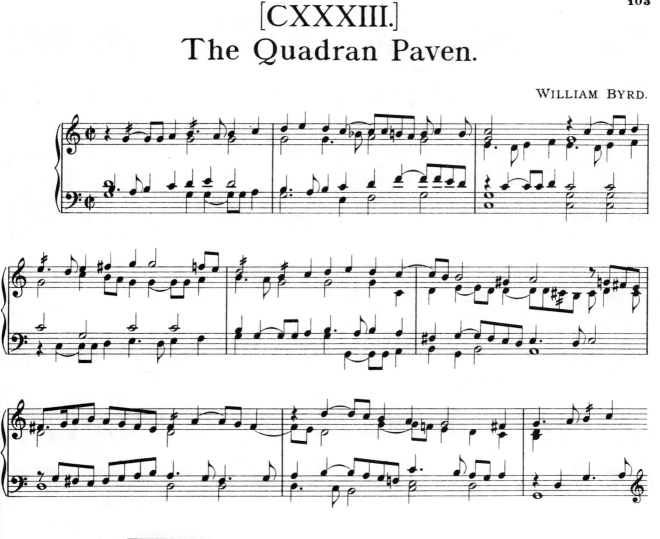

2 Rep.

* These two bars, the text of which is evidently corrupt, have been corrected from the version given in Will. Forster's Virginal Book in the Buckingham-Palace library.

Diese 2 offenbar entstellten Takte sind nach dem Exemplare dieses Stückes verbessert, das sich im Virginal Book des Will. Forster in der Bibliothek des Buckingham-Palace befindet.

* See note p. 104.
Siehe Anmerkung S. 104.

108

* Semiquavers in the M.S.
Sechzehntel in der Handschrift.

** The notes in brackets are indicated by "directs" in the previous line; they are not in the M.S.   [gedeutet.
Die in Klammern stehenden Noten fehlen in der Handschrift, sind aber am Ende der vorhergehenden Linie durch den Custos an-

* C sharp in the M. S.
  Cis in der Handschrift.

WILLIAM
BYRD.

* G in the M.S.
  G in der Handschrift.

** This bar is left blank in the M. S; it is supplied from Will. Forster's M. S.
Dieser Takt ist in der Handschrift nicht ausgefüllt; er ist nach Will. Forster's
Handschrift eingetragen.

[CXXXIV.]
Galiard to the Quadran Paven.

WILLIAM BYRD.

* Demisemiquavers in the M. S.
  Zweiunddreissigstel in der Handschrift.

* Demisemiquavers in the M.S.
Zweiunddreissigstel in der Handschrift.

* C sharp in the M.S.
  Cis in der Handschrift.

WILLIAM
BYRD.

* $\frac{A}{F}$ in the M. S.   * $\frac{A}{F}$ in der Handschrift.

[CXXXV.]
The King's Hunt.

JOHN BULL.

Rep.

Rep.

2

Rep.

Rep.

DOCTOR BULL.

* C sharp in the M.S.
  Cis in der Handschrift.

[CXXXVI.]
Pavana.

JOHN BULL.

Rep.

DOCTOR BULL.

[CXXXVII.]
Galiarda.

JOHN BULL.

Rep.

Rep.

DOCTOR BULL.

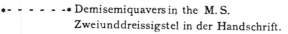

*------*Demisemiquavers in the M.S.
Zweiunddreissigstel in der Handschrift.

[CXXXVIII.]
Dr. Bull's Juell.

JOHN BULL.

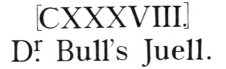

Rep.

Rep.

Rep.

DOCTOR BULL.

[CXXXIX.]
The Spanish Paven.

JOHN BULL.

DOCTOR BULL.

[CXL.]
In Nomine.
1.

[JOHN?] PARSONS.

PERSONS.

[CXLI.]
Wooddy-Cock.
2.

GILES FARNABY.

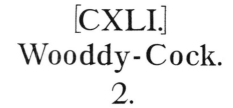

Rep.

Rep.

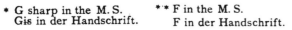

* G sharp in the M. S.   ** F in the M. S.
Gis in der Handschrift.   F in der Handschrift.

140

Rep.

2

Rep.

(#)

* E in M S.
E in der Handschrift.

Rep.

* G in the M.S.
  G in der Handschrift.

Rep.

— These two notes are not in the M.S., but are needed in order to complete the bar.
— Diese zwei Noten sind nicht im M.S. vorhanden, erscheinen aber nothwendig, um den Takt zu vervollständigen.

Rep.

Rep.

GILES
FARNABY.

[CXLII.]

The Duke of Brunswick's Alman.

JOHN BULL.

Rep.

Rep.

Rep. 2ª

DOCTOR BULL.

[CXLIII.]
Rosasolis.
12.

GILES FARNABY.

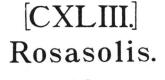

GILES
FARNABY.

[CXLIV.]
Psalme. [140.]
3.

J. P. SWEELINCK.

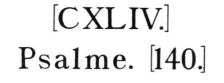

2ª Variatio.

3ª Variatio.

4ª Variatio.

* C sharp in the M S.
  Cis in der Handschrift.

5ª Variatio.

* B in the MS.
H in der Handschrift.

156

* E in the MS.
E in der Handschrift.

JEHAN PIETERSŌ SWELLING.

[CXLV.]

Alman.

ROBERT JOHNSON.

2

ROBERT JHONSON.

[CXLVI.]

Alman.

Robert Johnson.

Rob. Jhonsō.

[CXLVII.]

Alman.

ROBERT JOHNSON, set by GILES FARNABY.

ROBERT JHONSŌ sett by
GILES FARNABY.

[CXLVIII.]
The New Sa-Hoo.
13.

GILES FARNABY.

GILES FARNABY.

*- - * Demisemiquavers in the MS.
Zweiunddreissigstel in der Handschrift.

* A in the M.S.
A in der Handschrift.

[CXLIX.]
Nobodyes Gigge.

1.

RICHARD FARNABY.

* F in the M. S. by a mistake in the clef.
F in der Handschrift durch einen Schreibfehler.

Rep.

RICHARD FARNABY
soñe to GILES FARNABY.

* E in the M. S.
  E in der Handschrift.

[CL.]
Malt's come downe.

WILLIAM BYRD.

WILLIAM BYRD.

[CLI.]
Praeludium.

ANON.

[CLII.]
Alman.

THOMAS MORLEY.

Rep.

2

Rep.

THOMAS MORLEY.

[CLIII.]
Pavana.

THOMAS MORLEY.

174

2

*) G in the M.S.
   G in der Handschrift.

THOMAS MORLEY.

[CLIV.]
Galiarda.

THOMAS MORLEY.

* G in the M.S.
  G in der Handschrift.

Rep.

THOMAS MORLEY.

[CLV.]
La Volta.

WILLIAM BYRD.

WILLIAM BIRD.

[CLVI.]
Alman.

WILLIAM BYRD.

Rep.

3

Rep.

WILLIAM BYRD.

[CLVII.]
Wolseys Wilde.

WILLIAM BYRD.

WILLIAM BYRD.

[CLVIII.]
Callino Casturame.

WILLIAM BYRD.

WILLIAM BYRD.

[CLIX.]
La Volta.

T. MORLEY [set by] WILLIAM BYRD.

Rep.

WILLIAM BYRD.

[CLX.]
Rowland.

WILLIAM BYRD.

WILLIAM BYRD.

[CLXI.]
Why aske you.

ANON.

[CLXII.]
The Ghost.

WILLIAM BYRD.

Rep.

Rep.

WILLIAM BYRD.

* Crotchet in the M. S.
  Viertel in der Handschrift.

[CLXIII.]
Alman.

WILLIAM BYRD.

Rep.

2

Rep.

Rep.

Rep.

WILLIAM BYRD.

[CLXIV.]
Galliard.

WILLIAM BYRD.

WILLIAM BYRD.

[CLXV.]
Pavana.

WILLIAM BYRD.

*) B in the M.S.
H in der Handschrift.

WILLIAM BYRD.

[CLXVI.]
Galliarda.

WILLIAM BYRD.

Rep.

3

Rep.

4

Rep.

WILLAM BYRD.

[CLXVII.]
Pavana.*

WILLIAM BYRD.

* In the margin is written "the first t [hat] ever hee m [ade.]" The letters in brackets have been cut by the binder.
Eine Randbemerkung bezeichnet dieses Stück als die erste Pavana des Komponisten.

Rep.

WILLIAM BYRD.

[CLXVIII.]
Galiarda.

WILLIAM BYRD.

* Crotchet in the M. S.
  Viertel in der Handschrift.

WILLIAM BYRD.

* B natural in the M. S.   ** F sharp in the M. S.
H in der Handschrift.   Fis in der Handschrift.

[CLXIX.]
Pavana.

Thomas Morley.

Rep.

* F in the M. S.
  F in der Handschrift.

THOMAS MORLEY.

[CLXX.]
Galliarda.

THOMAS MORLEY.

Rep.

(♮)

THOMAS MORLEY.

[CLXXII.]
The Queenes Alman.

WILLIAM BYRD.

WILLIAM BYRD.

[CLXXIII.]
A Medley.

WILLIAM BYRD.

* A in the M.S.
  A in der Handschrift.

Rep.

Rep.

Rep.

Rep.

Rep.

WILLIAM BYRD.

[CLXXIV.]
Pavana.

WILLIAM BYRD.

WILLIAM BYRD.

[CLXXV.]
Galliarda.

WILLIAM BYRD.

WILLIAM BYRD.

[CLXXVI.]
Miserere.
3 Parts.

WILLIAM BYRD.

WILLIAM BYRD.

[CLXXVII.]
Miserere.
4 Parts.

WILLIAM BYRD.

WILLIAM BYRD.

* G sharp in the M. S.
Gis in der Handschrift.

[CLXXVIII.]
Pakington's Pownde.

ANON.

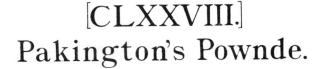

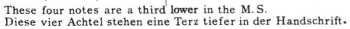

* *-----* These four notes are a third lower in the M. S. * G in the M. S.
Diese vier Achtel stehen eine Terz tiefer in der Handschrift. G in der Handschrift.

[CLXXIX.]
The Irishe Dumpe.

ANON.

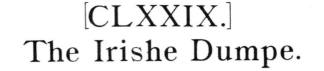

[CLXXX.]
Watkins Ale.

ANON.

[CLXXXI.]
A Gigg.

WILLIAM BYRD.

*In the margin of this piece are the letters "F. Tr." See Preface.
Am Rande dieses Stückes finden sich die Buchstaben „F. Tr." Siehe Vorrede.

* * B in M S.
H in der Handschrift.

[CLXXXII.]
Pipers Paven.

MARTIN PIERSON.

* Quaver rest in the M.S.   **F sharp in the M. S.
  Achtelpause in der Handschrift.   Fis in der Handschrift.

MARTIN PEERSON.

[CLXXXII.]
Piper's Galliard.

JOHN BULL.

Rep.

DOCTOR BULL.

* Quaver in the M.S.
  Achtel in der Handschrift.

[CLXXXIII.]
Variatio Ejusdem.

JOHN BULL.

* G in the MS.
  G in der Handschrift.

* From * to * stands a third higher in the M. S. owing to a mistake in the clef.
  Die Stelle von * bis * steht in der Handschrift infolge eines Irrthums hinsichtlich des Schlüssels eine Terz höher.

DOCTOR BULL.

- - - - - - Mistake in the change of clefs in the M. S.   * C in the M.S.
Schreibfehler in der Wechsel der Schlüssel im M.S.   C in der Handschrift.

[CLXXXIV.]
Praeludium. D.

JOHN BULL.

DOCTOR BULL.

[CLXXXV.]
Galiarda.

JOHN BULL.

Rep.

Rep.

*

(♮)

DOCTOR BULL.

(♮)   (♮)   (♮)

* D in the M. S.
   D in der Handschrift.

[CLXXXVI.]
Galiarda.

JOHN BULL.

— These notes are not in the M.S., probably by an oversight, and are supplied from the Berlin and Upsala MSS.
— Diese Noten sind nicht in der Handschrift wahrscheinlich aus Versehen, und werden nach MSS. zu Berlin und Upsala ergänzt

DOCTOR BULL.

[CLXXXVII.]
Allemanda.

MARCHANT

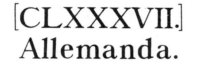

Rep.

MARCHANT.

[CLXXXVIII.]
Can shee.

ANON.

[CLXXXIX.]
A Gigge.
Doctor Bull's my selfe.

JOHN BULL.

DOCTOR BULL.

[CXC.]
A Gigge.

JOHN BULL.

DOCTOR BULL.

[CXCI.]
Sr. Jhon Grayes Galiard.

W. B.

W. B.

[CXCII.]
Preludium.

JOHN BULL.

DOCTOR BULL.

[CXCIII.]
A Toy.

ANON.

[CXCIV.]
Giles Farnaby's Dreame.

* Semiquaver in the M.S.
Sechzehntel in der Handschrift.

GILES FARNABY.

[CXCV.]
His Rest.
Galiard.

GILES FARNABY.

GILES FARNABIE.

[CXCVI.]
His Humour.

GILES FARNABY.

GILES FARNABY.

*A in the M.S.
A in der Handschrift.

[CXCVII.]
Fayne would I Wedd.

RICHARD FARNABY.

RICHARD FARNABYE.

[CXCVIII.]
A Maske.

GILES FARNABY.

GILES FARNABYE.

[CXCIX.]
A Maske.

GILES FARNABY.

GILES FARNABYE.

* A third higher in the M.S.
  Ein Terz höher in der Handschrift.

** Crotchet in the M.S.
  Viertel in der Handschrift.

[CC.]
An Almain.

ANON.

[CCI.]
Corranto.

ANON.

[CCII.]
Alman.

ANON.

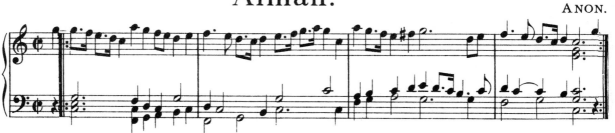

[CCIII.]
Corranto.

ANON.

[CCIV.]
Corranto.

ANON. (see Nº CXCIII.)

[CCV.]
Corranto.

ANON.

[CCVI.]
Daunce.

ANON.

* F sharp in the M.S.
  Fis in der Handschrift.

[CCVII.]
Worster Braules.

THOMAS TOMKINS.

THOMAS TOMKINS.

[CCVIII.]
Fantasia.

GILES FARNABY.

* B flat in the M.S.
 B in der Handschrift

---- See Preface.
    Siehe Vorrede.

GILES FARNABYE.

* A in the M.S.
  A in der Handschrift.

[CCIX.]
A Maske.

GILES FARNABY.

GILES FARNABYE

* G in the M.S.
  G in der Handschrift.

[CCX.]
Praeludium.

JOHN BULL.

DOCTOR BULL.

[CCXI.]

ANON.

[CCXII.]
Martin sayd to his man.

ANON.

[CCXIII.]
Almand.

WILLIAM TISDALL.

WILLIAM TISDALL.

[CCXIV.]
Pavana Chromatica.

Mrs Katherin Tregians Paven.

WILLIAM TISDALL.

WILLIAM TISDALL.

[CCXV.]
Ut, re, mi, fa, sol, la.

JOHN BULL.

287

* F in M. S.
F in der Handschrift.

DOCTOR BULL.

[CCXVI.]
Gipseis Round.

WILLIAM BYRD.

* The bass of this chord is E in the M.S.
  Im Bass steht E in der Handschrift.

*--*These two bars are divided unequally into three in the M.S.
  Diese zwei Takte sind in der Handschrift unregelmässiger Weise in drei eingetheilt.

** C in the M.S.
  C in der Handschrift.

---- Two bars in the M.S.
    Zwei Takte in der Handschrift.

* A in the M.S.
  A in der Handschrift.

WILLIAM BYRD.

[CCXVII.]
Fantasia.
4.

J. P. SWEELINCK.

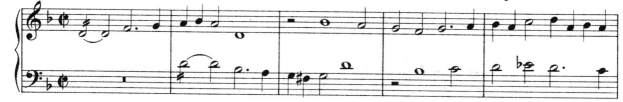

JHON PIETERSON SWEELING.
ORGANISTA A AMSTELREDA.

[CCXVIII.]
Coranto.

WILLIAM BYRD.

WILLIAM BYRD.

---- These bars arc divided into 3 bars of unequal value in the M.S.; the correct rhythm of the piece is indicated in the subsequent portion.
Diese Takte sind in der Handschrift in drei Takte von ungleichem Werth eingetheilt; der richtige Rhythmus des Stückes ist in dem nachfolgenden Theile angegeben.

[CCXIX.]
Pavana.
Clement Cottõ.
3.

WILLIAM TISDALL.

WILLIAM TISDALL.

[CCXX.]
Pavana.
4.

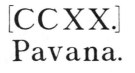

WILLIAM TISDALL.

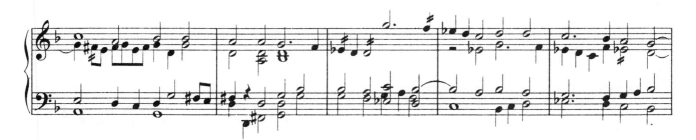

WILLIAM TISDALL.

[CCXXI.]
Coranto.

ANON.

[CCXXII.]
Alman.

HOOPER.

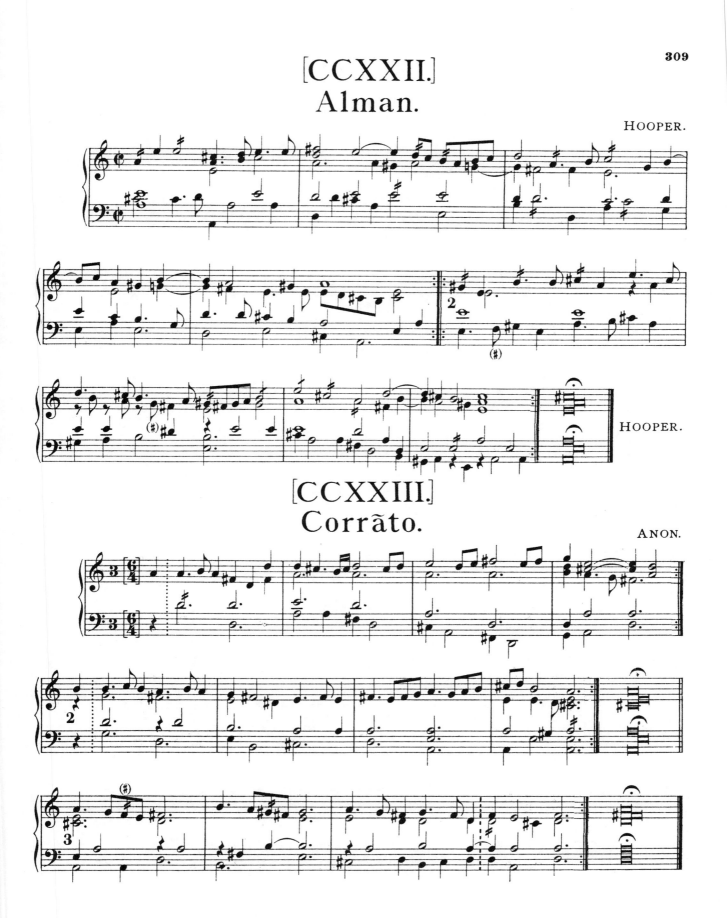

HOOPER.

[CCXXIII.]
Corrãto.

ANON.

[CCXXIV.]
Corranto.

ANON.

[CCXXV.]
Corrãto.

ANON.

* F in the M. S.
F in der Handschrift.

[CCXXVI.]
Corrāto.

ANON.

* For this A and F appear G and E in the M. S.
  Statt diesen A und F stehen in der Handschrift G und E.

[CCXXVII.]
Alman.

ANON.

[CCXXVIII.]
Corranto.

HOOPER.

HOOPER.

[CCXXIX.]
Fantasia.
20.

GILES FARNABY.

314

*) C sharp in the M.S.
Cis in der Handschrift.

GILES FARNABY.

[CCXXX.]
Loth to Depart.
21.

GILES FARNABY.

* G in the M.S.
  G in der Handschrift.

GILES FARNABY.

* Demisemiquavers in the M. S.
  Zweiunddreissigstel in der Handschrift.

[CCXXXI.]
Fantasia.
22.

GILES FARNABY.

GILES FARNABY.

[CCXXXII.]

23.

GILES FARNABY.

GILES FARNABY.

[CCXXXIII.]

24.*⁾

GILES FARNABY.

*) This piece is a transcription of "Ay me, poore heart", Nº 15 of Farnaby's canzonets.
   Dieses Stück ist eine Transcription von "Ay me, poore heart", Nr. 15 der Canzonetten von Farnaby.

GILES FARNABY.

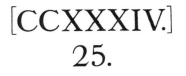

[CCXXXIV.]
25.

GILES FARNABY.

* E in M. S.
　E in der Handschrift.

** Demisemiquavers in the M. S.
　Zweiunddreissigstel in der Handschrift.

GILES FARNABY.

* C sharp in the M.S.
  Cis in der Handschrift.

[CCXXXV.]
Walter Erle's Paven.
26.

GILES FARNABY.

* Semiquavers in the M.S.
  Sechzehntel in der Handschrift.

Rep.

3

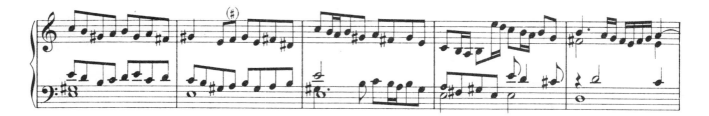

Rep.

GILES FARNABY.

[CCXXXVI.]
27.

GILES FARNABY.

* Demisemiquavers in the MS.
Zweiunddreissigstel in der Handschrift.

GILES FARNABY.

[CCXXXVII.]
Fantasia.
28.

GILES FARNABY.

GILES FARNABY.

[CCXXXVIII.]
Fantasia.
29.

GILES FARNABY.

* G sharp in the M.S.   ** A in the M.S.
Gis in der Handschrift.   A in der Handschrift.

348

GILES FARNABY.

[CCXXXIX.]
The L. Zouches Maske.
30.

GILES FARNABY.

* B in the M.S.
  H in der Handschrift.

Rep.

Rep.

GILES FARNABY.

[CCXL.]
Groũde.
31.

GILES FARNABY.

-- C- C sharp in the M.S.   ** Crotchet in the M S.
C- Cis in der Handschrift.   Viertel in der Handschrift.

* G sharp in the M.S.
  Gis in der Handschrift.

* C sharp in the M.S.
  Cis in der Handschrift.

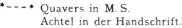

GILES FARNABY.

*- -*Quavers in the M. S.
Achtel in der Handschrift

[CCXLI.]
Coranto.

WILLIAM BYRD.

WILLIAM BYRD.

✻ Crotchet in M.S.
  Viertel in der Handschrift.

[CCXLII.]
Up T [ails] All.
32.

GILES FARNABY.

* C sharp in the M.S.
  Cis in der Handschrift.

* Semiquavers in the M.S.
  Sechzehntel in der Handschrift.

GILES FARNABY.

[CCXLIII.]
Jhonson's Medley.

EDWARD JOHNSON.

Rep.

2

Rep.

3

Rep.

EDWARD JHONSON.

[CCXLIV.]
Nowel's Galliard.

ANON.

Rep.

Rep.

Rep.

[CCXLV.]
Tower Hill.

GILES FARNABY.

GILES FARNABY.

[CCXLVI.]
Praeludium.
33.

GILES FARNABY.

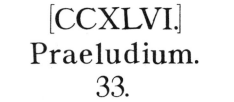

GILES FARNABY.

[CCXLVII.]
The King's Morisco.

ANON.

[CCXLVIII.]
A Duo.

RICHARD FARNABY.

RICHARD FARNABY.

[CCXLIX.]
Alman.

ANON.

[CCL.]
A Galliard Ground.
1.

WILLIAM INGLOT.

Rep.

378

Rep.

(♯)

Rep.

* Two quavers in the M.S.
 Zwei Achtel in der Handschrift.

WILLIAM INGLOT.

[CCLI.]
The Leaves bee greene.
2.

WILLIAM INGLOT.

382

WILLIAM INGLOT.

[CCLII.]
Pavana.

WILLIAM BYRD.

Rep.

Rep.

WILLIAM BYRD.

[CCLIII.]
Galiarda.

WILLIAM BYRD.

WILLIAM BYRD.

[CCLIV.]
Pavana.

WILLIAM BYRD.

Rep.

* B natural in the M. S.
  H in der Handschrift.

390

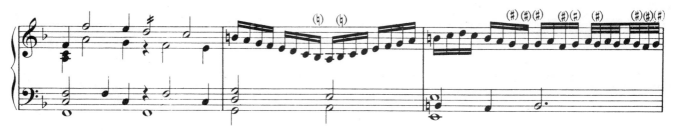

Rep.

[L. H.]

WILLIAM BYRD.

[CCLV.]
Galiarda.

WILLIAM BYRD.

WILLIAM BYRD.

[CCLVI.]
Pavana.

WILLIAM BYRD.

Rep.

Rep.

WILLIAM BYRD.

[CCLVII.]
Pavana Fant [asia].

WILLIAM BYRD.

Rep.

WILLIAM BYRD.

[CCLVIII.]
Galiarda.

WILLIAM BYRD.

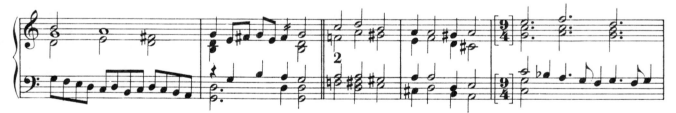

WILLIAM BYRD.

* Crotchet in the M S.
  Viertel in der Handschrift.

[CCLIX.]
The Earle of Oxfords Marche.

William Byrd.

WILLIAM BYRD.

[CCLX.]
Galiarda.
I.

JEHAN OYSTERMAYRE.

JEHAN OYSTERMAYRE.

* Quavers in the M.S.
  Achtel in der Handschrift.

** C in M.S.
   C in der Handschrift.

*** This A sharp is written as B flat in the M.S., and a sharp is prefixed to the B in the following bar.
   Dieses Ais steht als B in der Handschrift, ein Kreuz steht vor dem folgenden H.

[CCLXI.]
Fantasia.

WILLIAM BYRD.

* E D in the M S.
  E D in der Handschrift.

WILLIAM BYRD.

[CCLXII.]
The Duchesse of Brunswick's Toye.

JOHN BULL.

Rep.

Rep.

DOCTOR BULL.

[CCLXIII.]
A Toye.

ANON.

414

[CCLXIV.]
Corranto.

ANON.

[CCLXV.]
Corranto.
Lady Riche.

ANON.

[CCLXVI.]
Corranto.

ANON.

[CCLXVII.]
A Gigge.

GILES FARNABY.

GILES FARNABY.

[CCLXVIII.]
A Toy.

ANON.

Rep.

[CCLXIX.]
Galiarda.

GILES FARNABY.

Rep.

2

Rep.

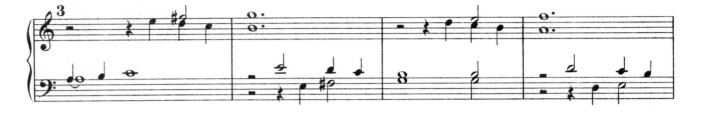

Rep.

GILES FARNABY.

[CCLXX.]
A Toye.

GILES FARNABY.

Rep.

Rep.

GILES FARNABY.

* A in the M.S.
A in der Handschrift.

[CCLXXI.]
The Primerose.

MARTIN PEERSON.

Rep.

2

Rep.

MARTIN PEERSON.

* Quavers in the M.S.
   Achtel in der Handschrift.

[CCLXXII.]
The Fall of the Leafe.

MARTIN PEERSON.

MARTIN PEERSON.

[CCLXXIII.]
Farnabye's Conceit.

GILES FARNABYE.

[CCLXXIV.]
Allemanda.

ANON.

Rep.

* D sharp in the M.S.
  Dis in der Handschrift.

[CCLXXV.]
Pavana.
Canon.
Two parts in one.

WILLIAM BYRD.

428

Rep.

* Semiquavers in the M.S.
  Sechzehntel in der Handschrift.

3

Rep.

WILLIAM BYRD.

[CCLXXVI.]
Pescodd Time.

WILLIAM BYRD.

10

11

WILLIAM BYRD.

[CCLXXVII.]
Pavana.
Delight.

EDWARD JOHNSON, set by WILLIAM BYRD.

Rep.

Rep.

EDWARD JHONSON
sett by
WILL. BYRD.

* Semiquavers in the M.S.
   Sechzehntel in der Handschrift.

[CCLXXVIII.]
Galiarda.

EDWARD JOHNSON, set by WILLIAM BYRD.

3

Rep.

ED. JHONSON.
sett by
WILLIAM BYRD.

[CCLXXIX.]
Miserere.
3 parts.

JOHN BULL.

2

DOCTOR BULL.

[CCLXXX.]
Tell mee, Daphne.

GILES FARNABY.

GILES FARNABY.

* Crotchet in the M. S.
 Viertel in der Handschrift.

[CCLXXXI.]
Mal Sims.

GILES FARNABY.

*F in the M S.
 F in der Handschrift.

GILES FARNABY.

[CCLXXXII.]
Munday's Joy.

JOHN MUNDAY.

MUNDAY.

* Quavers in the M. S.　**C in the M. S.
　Achtel in der Handschrift.　C in der Handschrift.

[CCLXXXIII.]
Rosseter's Galiard.

Set by GILES FARNABY.

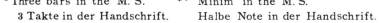

-- Three bars in the M. S.   ** Minim in the M. S.
3 Takte in der Handschrift.   Halbe Note in der Handschrift.

Rep.

3

Rep.

Sett by
GILES FARNABY

* Seniquavers in the M. S.   *˙* Demisemiquavers in the M. S.
  Sechzehntel in der Handschrift.   Zweiunddreissigstel in der Handschrift.

[CCLXXXIV.]

The Flatt Pavan.

GILES FARNABY.

Rep.

* Crotchets in the M. S.
  Viertel in der Handschrift.

Rep.

GILES FARNABY.

[CCLXXXV.]
Pavana.

GILES FARNABY.

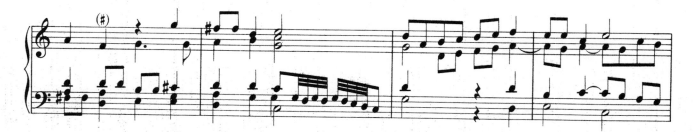

Rep.

* Demisemiquavers in the M. S.
  Zweiunddreissigstel in der Handschrift.

Rep.

GILES FARNABY.

* C♯ in the M. S.

Cis in der Handschrift.

[CCLXXXVI.]
Why aske you.

GILES FARNABY.

* Crotchet in the M. S.
  Viertel in der Handschrift.

Rep.

2

Rep.

GILES FARNABY.

*E in the M S.
 E in der Handschrift.

[CCLXXXVII.]
Farmer's Paven.

Giles Farnaby.

Rep.

* Quaver in the M. S.
  Achtel in der Handschrift.

Rep.

3

Rep.

* G sharp in the M. S.
  Gis in der Handschrift.

GILES FARNABY.

[CCLXXXVIII.]
Dalling Alman.

ANON.

[CCLXXXIX.]
The old Spagnoletta.

GILES FARNABY.

GILES
FARNABY.

* G in the M.S.
G in der Handschrift.

[CCXC.]
Lachrimæ Pavan.

JOHN DOWLAND, set by
GILES FARNABY.

Rep.

* Quaver in the M. S.   *·* Semiquavers in the M. S.
Achtel in der Handschrift.   Sechzehntel in der Handschrift.

Rep.

* This and the preceding note F appear as crotchets in the previous bar.
  Dieses E und das vorhergehende F stehen in der Handschrift als Viertel im vorhergehenden Takte.
** C in the M.S.
   C in der Handschrift.

Rep.

J. D. sett by
GILES FARNABY.

* Quavers in the M. S.
  Achtel in der Handschrift.

[CCXCI.]
Meridian Alman.

Set by GILES FARNABY.

Rep.

Sett by
GILES FARNABY.

[CCXCII.]
Pavana.

ORLANDO GIBBONS.

ORLANDO GIBBONS.

[CCXCIII.]
Muscadin.

GILES FARNABY.

* F in the M.S.
  F in der Handschrift.

GILES FARNABY.

[CCXCIV.]
Lady Montegle's Paven.

WILLIAM BYRD.

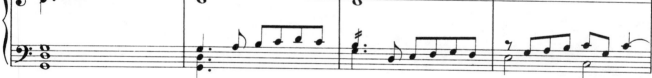

Rep.

WILLIAM BYRD.

* Crotchet in the M.S.
  Viertel in der Handschrift.

[CCXCV.]
Galiarda.
5.

WILLIAM TISDALL.

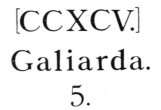

2

Rep.

* Crotchets in the M.S.
  Viertel in der Handschrift.

3

Rep.

WILLIAM TISDALL.

[CCXCVI.]
Fantasia.

GILES FARNABY.

* See Preface.
Siehe Vorrede.

* G sharp in the M.S.
  Gis in der Handschrift.

492

···) Semiquavers in the M.S.
Sechzehntel in der Handschrift.

GILES FARNABY.

[CCXCVII.]
Hanskin.

RICHARD FARNABY.

* C in the M.S.
  C in der Handschrift.

*) D in the M. S.
   D in der Handschrift.

Rep.

Rep.

* Semiquavers in the M.S.
  Sechzehntel in der Handschrift.

RICHARD FARNABY.

INDEX.